ZIMBABWE QUIZ

Basic Facts and Figures about Rhodesia

ISBN 0 904759 02 4

London 1975

International Defence and Aid Fund
104 Newgate Street, London EC1

Contents

The Smith regime introduced a decimal currency in 1970 based on the Rhodesian dollar; One Rhodesian dollar (1R$) equalled one South African rand equalled ten Rhodesian shillings. Subsequent currency changes have resulted in 1R$ = R1.19 = £0.72.

1.

Where is Rhodesia?

Rhodesia is a land locked territory in the geographical area known as Central Africa. The Zambezi serves as its northern border with Zambia whilst the Limpopo river in the south separates it from South Africa. To the south-west is the state of Botswana whilst on the east and north-east it is bordered by Mozambique. A map showing Rhodesia's position in Central and Southern Africa is on page 20.

2.

What is the population of Rhodesia?

6,100,000 in June 1973. It comprises:-

Africans	5,800,000	(95%)
Europeans	273,000	(4%)
Coloureds	19,500	(0.3%)
Asians	9,800	(0.2%)

The African population contains two main ethnic groupings: the Shona—approximately 71% and the Ndebele—approximately 15%. Coloureds are people of mixed race.

3.

What does Zimbabwe mean?

This is the African name for Rhodesia; it is intended to be the official name for the country when majority rule is achieved. Rhodesia is sometimes referred to as Southern Rhodesia —constitutionally this is still its official name.

The Zimbabwe ruins, near Fort Victoria, are an important and impressive indication of a precolonial civilisation which extended over much of central and south-east Africa.

The name Rhodesia, based on that of Cecil John Rhodes (see next question), is so closely associated with white settler colonial conquest that it is no longer acceptable to African opinion.

4.

When did the first white settlers arrive in Rhodesia?

In 1890 a small group of white settlers organized by Cecil Rhodes and known as the Pioneer Column marched into Mashonaland (the north and north eastern parts of Southern Rhodesia) from Bechuanaland (now Botswana). They set up camp at Harare (now Salisbury).

The British government had previously granted a Royal Charter to Rhodes' British South Africa Company entitling it to administer the area.

The African people resisted these and subsequent attempts to conquer and colonize their lands. In 1893 Rhodes attacked the Matabele with much loss of life on both sides. Then in 1896 and again in 1897 the Mashona and Matabele united to fight the invaders. But the white settlers were by then well entrenched and with the assistance of the British army successfully defeated the Africans.

The British South Africa Company administered the territory until 1923 when Britain granted the white settlers 'responsible self-government'.

5.

Why is Rhodesia different from other states in Africa?

Unlike the overwhelming majority of African states, Rhodesia is not ruled by the African majority but by the minority group of white settlers. Only South Africa and Namibia (South West Africa) are similarly under white minority rule.

Rhodesia was the only British colony in Africa which was never administered directly by the British colonial office; instead internal self-government was granted to the whites in 1923 following a period of company rule. (See question 4).

When Britain embarked on its policy of decolonization in Africa in the late 1950s and early '60s it was unwilling to grant independence to Rhodesia on the same basis as other African territories, i.e. African rule. The settlers, however, went even further and being already in effective control, demanded independence with no concessions towards African majority rule.

It was disagreements between the British government and both the white settler government and the African nationalists which formed the background to the unilateral declaration of independence by the Rhodesian regime, which was an illegal act. In law Rhodesia remains a British colony; the Smith regime is not officially recognised by any other state.

6.

What was U D I ?

The white settlers in Southern Rhodesia were originally granted "responsible self-government" by the United Kingdom in 1923 but in 1953 Southern Rhodesia joined with Northern Rhodesia (now Zambia) and Nyasaland (now Malawi) to form the Central African Federation.

Following the end of the Federation in 1963 and the gaining of independence by Malawi and subsequently Zambia, the white government in Rhodesia attempted to negotiate independence from the United Kingdom but refused to agree to a constitution which was acceptable to the African people.

The dispute continued until 11 November 1965 when the government led by Ian Smith, which was at that time the legal government of Rhodesia, unilaterally declared independence from the United Kingdom. At the same time they announced the introduction of the " 1965 Constitution " which whilst maintaining the basic features of the existing " 1961 Constitution " severed a number of remaining links with Britain.

7.

What was the response of the British government to UDI?

The British government denounced the declaration as an act of rebellion and dismissed Mr. Smith and his ministers.

Britain immediately introduced a variety of financial and trade sanctions against Rhodesia, and participated in a United Nations Security Council meeting on 12 November which condemned UDI and called upon all member states not to recognize or render assistance to the illegal regime. Subsequently further sanctions were imposed by the British government and the United Nations (see Question 62).

In October 1965 Mr. Wilson, the British Prime Minister, had categorically ruled out the use of force in the event of UDI. This gave rise to much criticism at the United Nations and from African states which drew a contrast between British practice in other colonial situations. Several states including Tanzania and Ghana severed diplomatic relations with Britain because of its failure to end the rebellion.

8.

Has the British government attempted to reach a settlement with the Smith regime?

Yes. On three different occasions detailed settlement proposals have been drawn up. The first negotiations were held on board *HMS Tiger* from 2—4 December 1966 but the proposals were rejected by Smith and his regime on his return to Salisbury. Then on 9—13 October 1968 Mr. Smith and Mr. Wilson again met; this time on board *HMS Fearless*. The proposals which emerged, under which it was calculated majority rule could not be achieved before 1999, were again rejected by the Smith regime. A third set of proposals were agreed during a visit by the British Foreign Secretary, Sir Alec Douglas-Home, to Salisbury in November 1971. The proposals were not implemented, because they failed the test of acceptability carried out by the Pearce Commission in early 1972. Under the 1971 proposals it was estimated that the earliest date that parity (i.e. an equal number of seats for Africans and Europeans in parliament) could be achieved would be 2035 A.D.

What are the " Six Principles "?

These are the principles laid down by the British government as the basic requirements for the granting of independence. They are:

1. The principle and intention of unimpeded progress to majority rule, already enshrined in the 1961 constitution, would have to be maintained and guaranteed.

2. There would also have to be guarantees against retrogressive amendment of the constitution.

3. There would have to be immediate improvement in the political status of the African population.

4. There would have to be progress towards ending racial discrimination.

5. The British government would need to be satisfied that any basis for independence was acceptable to the people of Rhodesia as a whole.

6. It would be necessary to ensure that, regardless of race, there was no oppression of majority by minority or of minority by majority.

The sixth principle was added by the British government in January 1966 following UDI.

What is NIBMAR?

No Independence Before Majority African Rule. This has been the policy of the African nationalist groups within Rhodesia and is supported by the Organisation of African Unity and the vast majority of the member states of the United Nations. Following the failure of the " Tiger " talks the British government temporarily accepted NIBMAR because of undertakings given to the Commonwealth Conference of September 1966. But in general successive British governments have preferred to base their approach on the " Six Principles " (see Question 9) which fall short of majority rule before independence.

11.

What did the Pearce Commission find?

The Commission was appointed by the British government to test the acceptability of the settlement terms agreed between Sir Alec Douglas-Home and Ian Smith in November 1971. All the members of the Commission, with the exception of the chairman Lord Pearce and one vice-chairman Lord Harlech, were serving or former British colonial officials. It was compelled by the strength of African opposition to the settlement terms to conclude that they were unacceptable to the population as a whole.

12.

Who, *de facto*, governs Rhodesia?

The Smith regime which illegally declared independence in 1965. It is composed of members or supporters of the all-white Rhodesian Front, which dominates the House of Assembly, and has the overwhelming support of the white population.

13.

What constitution operates, *de facto*, in Rhodesia today?

The " 1969 Constitution " by which Rhodesia declared itself a Republic, and which came into operation on 2 March 1970. Under this Constitution a President appointed by the Executive Council is the Head of State and the Legislature consists of the Head of State and a Parliament comprising a Senate and House of Assembly.

Senate: A 23-member body consisting of:

- (a) 10 European members elected by an electoral college of European members of the House of Assembly;
- (b) 10 African chiefs elected by the Council of Chiefs;
- (c) 3 persons (increased in 1974 to 5) of any race appointed by the Head of State.

House of Assembly: A 66-member body consisting of:

- (a) 50 Europeans elected by the European electorate;
- (b) 8 Africans elected by registered African voters;
- (c) 8 Africans elected by eight tribal electoral colleges.

This Constitution permanently rules out the possibility of majority rule. It allows for the number of African MPs to be increased as the African population contributes a greater percentage of taxes until parity is reached between the two racial groups in the House of Assembly. One academic economist has estimated that this will take over 1,000 years.

14.

What is the state of the different parties in the Rhodesian House of Assembly?

In the 1974 general election all 50 European seats were won by the Rhodesian Front who secured 75% of the European votes cast. The eight Africans selected by the tribal electoral colleges are all members of the Rhodesian Electoral Union. Of the eight elected African MPs only one was not an independent. He was a Centre Party candidate but shortly after the election he resigned from the Centre Party and joined with the others in a group of pro-ANC independents.

The Rhodesian Front has been in power since 1962 and under the existing system there is no likelihood of it being defeated by any other parliamentary party.

15.

Can all Africans vote in parliamentary elections?

No. The franchise qualifications based on income, property

and education exclude the vast majority of Africans and automatically rise as the cost of living rises. Because of dissatisfaction with the present and previous constitutions many Africans refuse to register and vote. Only 2,362 Africans voted in the 1974 General Election, out of a total of nearly six million.

The official claim is that the eight tribal electoral colleges, which consist of all the chiefs, headmen and elected councillors in their area, represent the interests of Africans who do not qualify to vote. (See also Question 37).

16.
Are Africans free to participate in political affairs?

No. The political rights of the African people are systematically denied by specific legislation, by emergency regulations and by the day-to-day actions of the army, police and employees of the Ministry of Internal Affairs.

The major items of legislation are:
(i)   The Unlawful Organizations Act, 1959. This has been used to ban successive African nationalist parties. The Zimbabwe African People's Union (ZAPU) was banned in September 1963 and the Zimbabwe African National Union (ZANU) in 1964.
(ii)   The Law and Order (Maintenance) Act, 1960 as amended. This is the cornerstone of Rhodesian security legislation, and provides powers to prohibit meetings, publications, processions and to restrict people to a designated area. It also covers offences such as " intimidation ", " terrorism " and sabotage.
(iii)   The Emergency Powers Act, 1960. This empowers the President to declare a state of emergency; a 3-month state of emergency was proclaimed on 5 November 1965 and has been continuously renewed. Emergency Powers Regulations have been made on many occasions since then to curtail political rights.
(iv)   The African Affairs Act, 1928 as amended. This has been used to ban all political meetings in Tribal Trust Lands and to punish and depose African chiefs who resist government policy.

17.

What political rights have Asians and Coloureds?

Asians and Coloureds are classified under the 1969 constitution as European for the purpose of parliamentary representation but there are no Coloureds or Asians in the House of Assembly. During 1974 parliament was in the process of amending the Constitution so that the number of appointed members in the Senate would be increased from three to five. There was considerable speculation that these two additional places would be filled by a member of each of the Coloured and Asian communities.

18.

What legal political parties exist in Rhodesia?

The Rhodesian Front: founded in June 1961, it has been the ruling party since 1962. In the General Election of 1974 the Rhodesian Front polled 75% of the European votes and won all 50 seats.

The Rhodesian Party: the major opposition party to the Rhodesian Front in the 1974 General Election; it polled 19% of the votes but failed to win a single seat.

The Centre Party: a multi-racial party whose only successful candidate in the 1974 General Election resigned from the Centre Party shortly afterwards to work with the group of pro-ANC African MPs.

In addition there are a number of ultra-right groupings such as the Rhodesia Group which fielded seven candidates in the 1974 General Election, and the Rhodesian National Party.
No major legal African political parties exist. The African Progressive Party contested the 1974 General Election but only succeeded to obtain a total of 79 votes in the five seats it contested. The African MPs selected by the tribal electoral colleges are members of the Rhodesian Electoral Union.

19.

What are the main objectives of the Rhodesian Front?

Professor Claire Palley, formerly a lecturer in law at University College Rhodesia, has written that judging by the laws the Rhodesian Front has introduced since 1963 they are:

(a) to perpetuate European political power indefinitely;

(b) to strengthen European domination of the administrative and legislative machinery of government;

(c) to maintain police control in order to curtail African political resistance to the status quo;

(d) to confer economic benefits on whites at the expense of Africans;

(e) to re-introduce social segregation between the races in places where the racial groups have contact.

20.

Is there censorship in Rhodesia?

Yes. Under the Censorship and Entertainments Control Act a Censorship Board was established in December 1967 to control literature and entertainment in Rhodesia. The Board has banned a large number of political publications. The Censorship Board has also banned pornography and certain forms of entertainment; for example in 1974 it prevented a discotheque being opened in a Salisbury township.

21.

How is the press affected by censorship?

Government censorship of newspapers was introduced at UDI but lifted in April 1968. Since then a policy of voluntary censorship has existed. According to a former Secretary for Law and Order the Argus press, the major newspaper publishers, has always co-operated with the regime when asked not to publish an item for " security reasons ". In addition the

1969 Emergency Powers (Sanctions Counter-Espionage) Regulations and the Official Secrets Act prevent the publication of any material which could lead to the disclosure of sanctions-breaking. Publication of the proceedings of trials can be restricted by the Minister of Justice under Section 403A of the Criminal Code.

Newspapers which have been sympathetic to the African nationalist cause have been banned. In August 1964 a Thomson Group newspaper with a mainly African readership, the *Daily News*, was banned under Section 18 of the Law and Order Maintenance Act. In the autumn of 1974 a Catholic weekly paper *Moto* was banned, initially for three months but subsequently permanently.

22.

Is there a State of Emergency in Rhodesia?

Yes. A state of emergency was declared by the Governor of Rhodesia at the request of the Rhodesian Front government on 5 November 1965, just six days before UDI. It has been in force continuously since that date.

23.

What powers does the existence of a State of Emergency give to the Rhodesian authorities?

The Emergency Powers Act of 1960 allows the government to declare a State of Emergency either throughout the whole country (as has existed since 1965) or in particular areas.

During the period of a State of Emergency the Act empowers the government to make Emergency Powers Regulations. Such regulations have been used to control many features of life in Rhodesia including security, labour, the economy and trade. Important examples of these regulations are:
● The Emergency Powers (Maintenance of Law and Order) Regulations which provide powers to detain people;

● The Emergency Powers (Control of Manpower) Regulations which control the activities of employees in controlled industries;

● The Emergency Powers (Prohibition of Foreign Aid to Designated Political Parties) Regulations which were introduced to prevent funds being provided to the African National Council from abroad;

● The Emergency Powers (Sanctions Counter-Espionage) Regulations which exist to prevent anyone disclosing information about sanctions breaking.

24.

Are people detained without trial in Rhodesia?

Numerous political opponents of the regime have been detained without trial under Emergency Powers Regulations and the Law and Order (Maintenance) Act. In December 1974 Mr Smith announced that African nationalist detainees and restrictees (then thought to number about 400) were to be released in terms of an agreement reached in Lusaka earlier that month (see Questions 25 and 55). At the time of writing (January 1975) it appeared that less than a quarter had actually been released.

25.

What does it mean if somebody is restricted?

Under the Law and Order (Maintenance) Act the Minister of Law and Order is able to restrict a person to a particular area. These powers have been used repeatedly since the early sixties to curb the activities of African nationalists. Many have been sent, like Joshua Nkomo, to restricted areas. Others have been restricted to their home district or barred from going within a certain distance of the centre of Salisbury. Restricted persons may not be named or quoted in the press or other media.

In terms of the agreement reached in Lusaka in December

1974 involving representatives of the Smith regime and members of the re-constituted African National Council (see Question 52) restrictees—like detainees—were supposed to be released. On 19 January 1975 the Rhodesian Minister of Law and Order announced that the release of restrictees and detainees had been halted.

26.

Are there any restraints on the right of freedom of assembly in Rhodesia?

Yes. Public meetings, defined as any group of twelve people, can only be held if a permit is obtained fourteen days in advance from the relevant local authority and the police. Under the African Affairs Act a district commissioner can prohibit individuals from holding or addressing meetings in African Purchase Areas or Tribal Trust Lands. According to the Ministry of Internal Affairs, in fact, in the Tribal Trust Lands all meetings outside the tribal system are prohibited.

In urban areas there are numerous cases of permission for meetings being refused by local authorities or of large deposits being demanded, which effectively prevents the meeting from taking place.

Other restraints include a total ban on open-air, evening and Sunday meetings. Specific individuals can be prohibited from attending public gatherings by order of the Minister of Law and Order. It is also a criminal offence to picket.

27.

Is there any evidence of police brutality or torture in Rhodesia?

Yes. It has been repeatedly claimed that the police and other security forces employ techniques of torture in order to elicit information. There have been many instances of defendants in trials stating that they had been forced to make statements under torture; examples given include the use of electric shocks, electric " snake " torture and beatings. Apart from specified tortures, incidents of general brutality have also occurred. In August 1974 church leaders published ten well-documented cases of brutality by the Rhodesian security forces against Africans, and later legal action was brought against the Minister of Law and Order.

28.

Are there passes in Rhodesia as there are in South Africa?

Yes. All Africans over 16, (and in certain areas over 12), are required to carry a registration or identity certificate at all times (the only exemptions being for Africans living legally in Tribal Trust Lands within the recognized area of their own village).

These certificates are required under the African (Registration and Identification) Act which in its present form became law in January 1973. This reinforcement of the pass laws reversed a period of relaxation at the time of the Central African Federation.

Under the Vagrancy Act, Africans classified as " vagrants " can be prohibited from entering urban areas; their certificates are endorsed with particulars of their banning order. A " vagrant " includes anyone in an urban area who is not lawfully resident in that area or who is not employed by such a person.

A programme of re-registration began in November 1973 with the issuing of registration books which for the first time contained the holders' photograph. Re-registration was restricted to districts in the north-east of Rhodesia where pass exemptions referred to above do not apply.

29.

Is racial segregation practised in Rhodesia?

There are few aspects of life in Rhodesia which racial segrega-

tion does not affect. It is enforced by law for:
    (a)   political representation;
    (b)   allocation of land;
    (c)   housing in urban areas;
    (d)   primary and secondary education;
    (e)   police and military service;
    (f)   health services.

In practice racial segregation also applies in employment, entertainment and most sporting activities.

30.

Are people free to live where they wish in Rhodesia?

No. Soon after the white settlers first arrived in Rhodesia they set aside reserves for the Africans. In 1930 with the introduction of the Land Apportionment Act segregation of land was legally enforced. Most of the country was divided into mutually exclusive European and African areas. The Land Tenure Act, 1969, which replaced the Land Apportionment Act, included provision for the removal of various pockets of African land surrounded by European land.

Various attempts have been made to prevent Coloureds and Asians from living in European areas despite their official classification as Europeans under the 1969 constitution. In December 1972 the Deeds Act was amended to allow restrictive conditions to be included in title deeds for property.

31.

What percentage of land is allocated to Africans?

An equal amount of land, 45 million acres, is allocated to the Africans and the Europeans. An additional 6 million acres is designated as National Land (game reserves etc.). Of the 45 million acres allocated to Africans, Tribal Trust Lands comprise 39.9 million acres and African Purchase Areas 3.7 million acres.

The display of maps inside front and back covers indicate how the land allocated to Europeans includes all the towns, main road and rail links and additionally the areas with most favourable climatic conditions.

Fig I. Land Allocation & Population.

Europeans

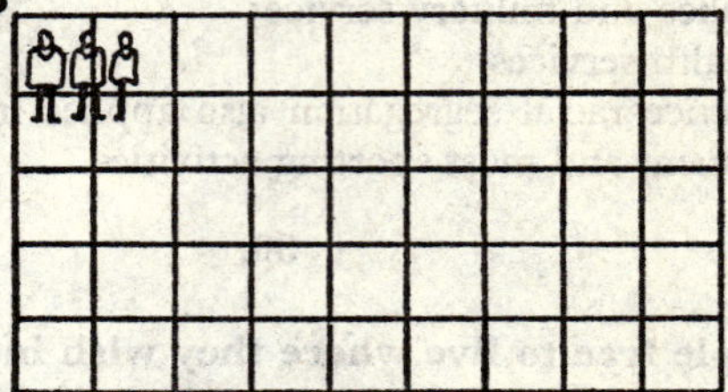

Land: 45 million acres
Population: 273,000

Africans

Land: 45 million acres
Population: 5,800,000

Key: Each figure represents 100,000 people
Each square   "   "   1 million acres

Under what conditions are Africans allowed to live in European areas?

All the towns in Rhodesia are in European areas. The general policy of successive governments has been to allow Africans to live in urban areas only if they are in employment. Two types of accommodation have been provided for African workers: locations which house " unmarried workers " and urban townships where families are allowed to live. Various laws govern African residence in urban areas; the African (Urban Areas) Accommodation and Registration Act for example makes it illegal for the family of an African domestic servant to live with him in a European suburb without official permission. During the period of the Central African Federation certain improvements were made in the conditions; for example Africans could acquire houses on leasehold, but this trend has been reversed since the election of the Rhodesian Front.

Legislation introduced in 1972 empowers district commissioners to " endorse out ", i.e. expel Africans from urban areas unless they are lawfully resident or employed in the area. The Smith regime is now considering plans for the provision of townships in the Tribal Trust Lands from which Africans will have to commute daily to work in European areas.

33.

What is urban life like for the Africans?

The townships are overcrowded and in many cases are squalid slums. In many there is no domestic electricity, water has to be fetched from a tap in the street and sanitary facilities are very primitive. Few entertainment and recreational facilities exist (except municipally-owned beerhalls) and schools and other social services are inadequate. The townships are designed strategically: water and electricity can be cut off in the event of strikes or political demonstrations.

In Salisbury there is a small township called Marimba Park where a small number of African families own European-style houses; it is regularly inspected by overseas visitors.

34.

Why do Africans remain in the urban areas if life is so bad there?

For several reasons. Firstly because it is the only place where there is a chance of earning a living; nearly all the country's industry and commerce is in the urban areas. Secondly the Tribal Trust Lands are so poor and overcrowded that they cannot support even their present population. Thirdly, because the whites need cheap African labour, they have introduced a system of laws and taxation which forces Africans to enter into the cash economy and work in the whites' industry and trade. Finally many Africans are now urban-born and have no other home.

35.

Are there Bantustans in Rhodesia?

No. But a policy of " provincialization " is being implemented which contains many features of the South African Bantustan policy. This policy, first announced by the Rhodesian Front in July 1972, involves the delegation of greater local government powers to tribal authorities. In each of the seven provinces of Rhodesia there is to be a Regional Authority consisting of one chief from each administrative district in the province appointed by the provincial Assembly of Chiefs and two additional members, one chosen from the chairmen of the African Councils in the Tribal Trust Lands and the other from the chairmen of the African Councils in the African Purchase Areas. These Regional Authorities would be responsible for projects such as dam building, road improvement and the administration of certain aspects of educational and other social services.

The first two Regional Authorities in Mashonaland South and Matabeleland North held their inaugural meetings in January 1974.

36.

What is the difference between the Tribal Trust Lands and African Purchase Areas?

In the African Purchase Areas land can be acquired by individual Africans whilst in the Tribal Trust Lands the land is owned in common. According to the 1969 census there were 2,911,040 Africans in Tribal Trust Lands (TTLs) but only 132,810 Africans in African Purchase Areas (APAs). In practice the TTLs are predominantly subsistence agriculture, whereas farming for cash economy predominates in the APAs. The APAs usually have no chiefs or headmen and local affairs are administered by local African Councils. Councils also exist in the TTLs but these are dominated by the government-appointed chiefs or headmen.

Areas in the Tribal Trust Lands can be expropriated from the Africans without compensation in the event of a mining claim being established. Mining speculators, who are free to prospect in the TTLs, are able to make compulsory purchase of any land required for mining development.

37.

What is the role of the African chiefs?

They were traditionally the leaders of the African people and in many cases led the resistance to European colonization in the 19th century. The role of the chiefs has subsequently changed dramatically; they are now appointed and paid by the government and particularly following the coming to power of the Rhodesian Front they have been used as instruments to implement government policy.

There are many well documented cases of chiefs who have resisted this role being deposed or fined and imprisoned. The Council of Chiefs has been used to support and justify government policy, particularly at the time of UDI and the visit of the Pearce Commission. Partly because of this, and also (in Shona-speaking areas) because of the fact that the chiefs are

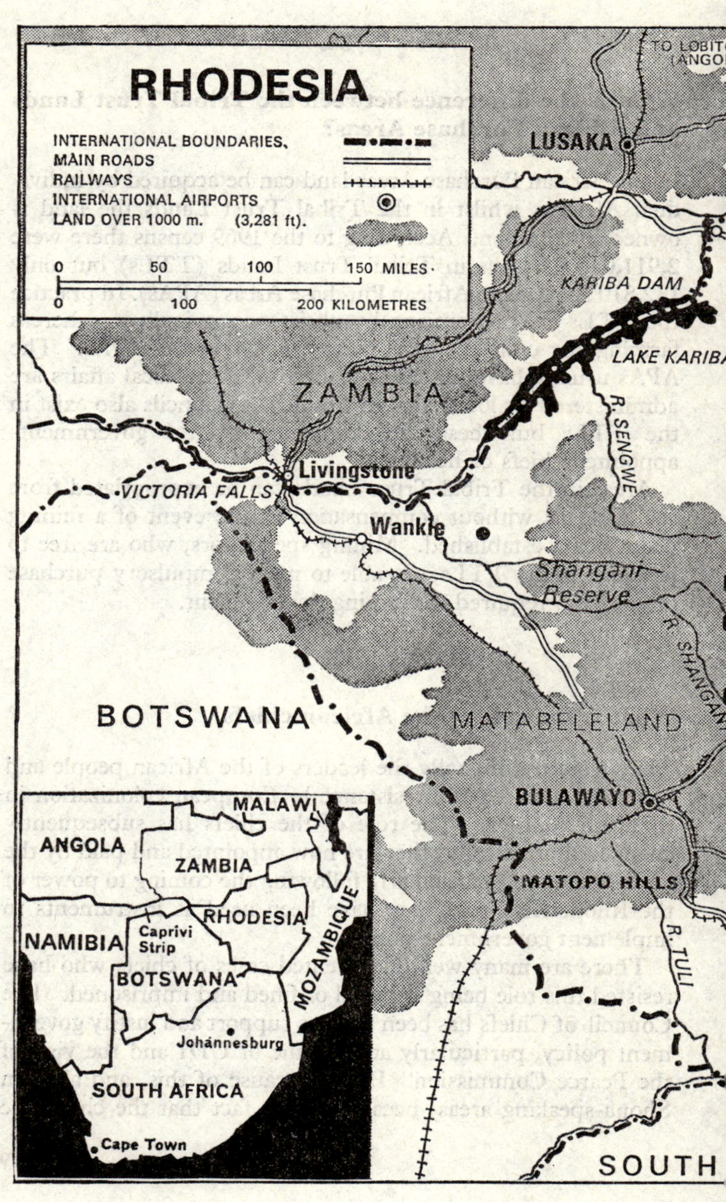

RHODESIA
INTERNATIONAL BOUNDARIES,
MAIN ROADS
RAILWAYS
INTERNATIONAL AIRPORTS
LAND OVER 1000 m.   (3,281 ft).
0   50   100   150 MILES
0   100   200 KILOMETRES
TO LOBITO
(ANGOLA)
LUSAKA
KARIBA DAM
LAKE KARIBA
ZAMBIA
R. SENGWE
Livingstone
VICTORIA FALLS
Wankie
Shangani Reserve
R. SHANGANI
BOTSWANA
MATABELELAND
BULAWAYO
MATOPO HILLS
R. TULI
SOUTH
MALAWI
ANGOLA
ZAMBIA
RHODESIA
Caprivi Strip
NAMIBIA
MOZAMBIQUE
BOTSWANA
Johannesburg
SOUTH AFRICA
Cape Town

30°E
34°
R. ZAMBEZI
R. HUNYANI
ndu
Sinoia
SALISBURY
VUMBA MTS.
oma
Hartley
MASHONALAND
Umtali
CHIMANIMANI MTS.
Beira
MELSETTER UPLANDS
Ft. Victoria
KYLE DAM
Zimbabwe Ruins
R. SABI
MOZAMBIQUE
R. LUNDI
R. NUANETSI
BANGALA DAM
R. SAVE
Beitbridge
R. LIMPOPO
AFRICA
N

usually very old and uneducated, they have now lost most of their former standing in African society.

38.

Is segregation applied to schools in Rhodesia?

Yes. There are separate schools for each racial group, Africans, Coloureds, Asians and Europeans.

39.

Is this segregated education equal for all races?

No. The standard for Africans is much inferior.
● School is compulsory for all European children but not for Africans. In fact 60% of African children have to leave school before the end of their primary education and only 0.2% reach the VIth form.
● There is extreme overcrowding in African schools; double sessions have become common practice because of the shortage of classrooms, schools and teachers.

Fig 2. Enrolments in African Primary & Secondary Education, 1974

● In the year 1972-3 the regime allocated R$20.1 million for the education of 69,901 European, Asian and Coloured school children; the amount allocated for 788,071 Africans was R$21.8 million.

● Whilst the parents of European children pay little or no school fees, African parents have to pay for stationery, most text books and also to contribute to school funds. This problem is particularly acute in secondary education where many rural schools of necessity are boarding schools. For most parents the fees are almost prohibitive.

40.

But isn't the University of Rhodesia multiracial?

Yes, in that both African and European students attend the University; but in practice racial discrimination impinges on many aspects of the University's life. In the summer of 1973 protests against racial practices at the University led to the imprisonment of over 100 African students.

Since UDI there have been a number of cases of lecturers being deported or being prevented from taking up appointments by being declared prohibited immigrants.

41.

Does the illegal regime encourage immigration to Rhodesia?

Yes, but white immigrants only. They do so because there is a growing shortage of skilled white labour and because many young whites are leaving Rhodesia.

Immigration campaigns are declining in success; net immigration into Rhodesia has fallen from 9,400 in 1971 to 1,680 in 1973. A massive Settlers '74 campaign which aimed to collect the names and addresses of a million prospective settlers only succeeded in obtaining 42,000 names.

Immigration of Coloureds or Asians is usually not allowed.

Foreign Africans are allowed to enter Rhodesia for employment but the numbers involved have fallen dramatically during the last decade (see Question 49).

42.

What happens to immigrants or foreigners who disagree with the policies of the regime?

They can be deported. These powers have been used extensively against journalists, missionaries and university lecturers. The regime can also declare a person a prohibited immigrant and thus prevent him from entering the country.

The 1970 Citizens Act enables the regime to deprive of their citizenship persons who obtained it by registration (i.e. not by birth). By use of these powers the regime has been able to deport some of its own citizens.

Fig 3. Employment by Race, 1973

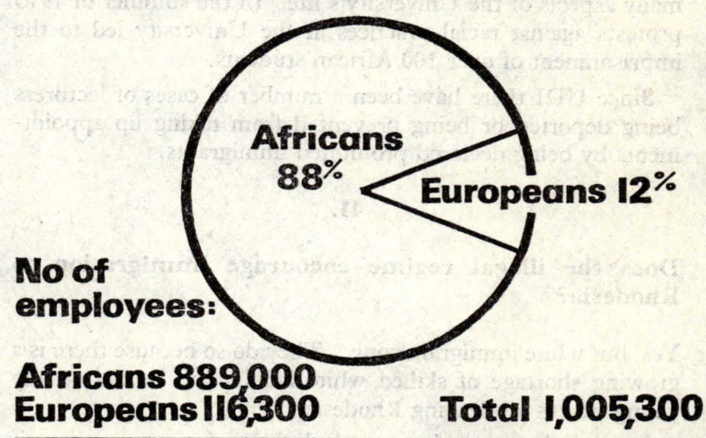

43.

Do Africans and Europeans receive equal pay in Rhodesia?

No. The average income per employee for Europeans during

1973 was R$3,901. For African employees the average income was R$359. The gap between average European and African wages has increased from R$2,809 in 1970 to R$3,542 in 1973.

Fig 4. Earnings by Race, 1973

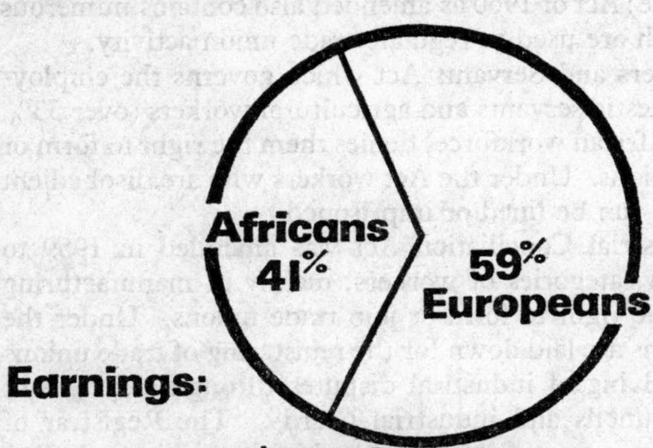

44.

Are African wages sufficient to live on?

No. A poverty datum line unit at the University of Rhodesia calculated the income required for families of various sizes to live at the poverty datum line (i.e. minimum subsistence level).

The unit found that in January 1974 in Salisbury the average family had six members who would require an income of over R$70 per month. In fact over 90% of Africans employed in towns and mines were earning less than R$70 per month.

Can Africans join trade unions?

The rights of Africans to organize in trade unions are restricted by complex legal constraints. The major items of legislation are the Masters and Servants Act of 1901 and the Industrial Conciliation Act of 1934 as amended. The Law and Order (Maintenance) Act of 1960 as amended also contains numerous powers which are used to regulate trade union activity.

The Masters and Servants Act which governs the employment of domestic servants and agricultural workers (over 53% of the total African workforce) denies them the right to form or join trade unions. Under the Act workers who are disobedient or neglectful can be fined or imprisoned.

The Industrial Conciliation Act was amended in 1959 to allow certain categories of workers, mainly in manufacturing and trade, the right to form or join trade unions. Under the Act conditions are laid down for the registering of trade unions and the resolving of industrial disputes through a system of industrial councils and industrial boards. The Registrar of Trade Unions is vested with wide arbitary powers including the right to refuse to register a trade union. The system of industrial councils and boards is similarly weighted heavily in favour of the government and employers.

The Act, whilst allowing for multi-racial unions, provides for the establishment of racially segregated unions and even in the multi-racial unions voting rights are defined so as to guarantee white workers' domination. The Act also makes the establishment of general unions, i.e. unions catering for workers in several industries, illegal.

The overall effect of this legislation is to make it virtually impossible for African trade unions to function. In 1971 it was estimated that only 5.2% of the total urban African workforce was represented by registered trade unions.

Are African workers allowed to strike?

Rhodesian labour and security laws make it virtually impossible for African workers to hold a lawful strike. The Masters and Servants Act, which governs the employment of domestic servants and agricultural workers, makes any act of disobedience an indictable offence. It is a criminal offence for anyone to be involved in strike action in " essential services " which are defined so broadly that few areas of employment are not included.

Many other restrictions exist. The Law and Order (Maintenance) Act makes it illegal to picket, controls the organisation of trade union meetings and even makes it an offence, with a penalty of ten years' imprisonment "to boo. . . anyone who has not joined a strike with you ".

In practice many trade unionists have been detained or restricted, the Unlawful Organisations Act has been used to ban trade unions and the police have brutally suppressed strikes by African workers.

47.

Is unemployment a problem in Rhodesia?

Yes. It is estimated that tens of thousands of urbanized Africans are unemployed. This huge reserve of labour allows employers to pay starvation wages with the sure knowledge that if their workers strike, they can simply be replaced.

48.

Are Africans able to develop their skills through apprenticeships?

In principle yes, but in practice no. The Apprenticeship Act of 1959 allowed African apprenticeship for the first time but despite an acute shortage of skilled workers in December 1971 out of 2,181 apprentices only 59 were Africans.

Are there many foreign Africans in Rhodesia?

At the time of the 1969 census there were nearly 300,000 foreign Africans in Rhodesia, including 163,440 from Malawi and 109,110 from Mozambique. 34% of all adult African employees were foreign workers. The number of Africans entering Rhodesia has fallen dramatically during the last two decades. In 1955 there were 110,970 foreign African immigrants; in 1973 there were 11,310.

What is ZAPU?

ZAPU is the Zimbabwe African People's Union which was founded in December 1961 and is officially recognized by the Organisation of African Unity and the United Nations as a liberation movement seeking majority rule and independence for Zimbabwe (Rhodesia). Its president is Joshua Nkomo who was restricted from 1964 until his release in December 1974. ZAPU was the successor to the National Democratic Party, which was banned in December 1961. ZAPU itself was banned on 19 September 1962 under the Unlawful Organizations Act.

For a short period, until August 1964, ZAPU leaders regrouped to form the People's Caretaker Council, while maintaining and developing the ZAPU structure underground. Many ZAPU members have been imprisoned or restricted. ZAPU guerilla units have been active inside Rhodesia since UDI, especially in the west and north-west.

In December 1974 a unity agreement was signed by the four Zimbabwe African nationalist organisations (ZAPU, ZANU, FROLIZI† and the ANC) by which they united in the re-constituted African National Council.

† FROLIZI, the Front for the Liberation of Zimbabwe, was founded in 1971 by former members of ZAPU and ZANU.

51.

What is ZANU?

ZANU is the Zimbabwe African National Union which was founded in August 1963 under the leadership of the Rev. Ndabaningi Sithole who together with some other ZAPU leaders, broke away from ZAPU partially as a result of disagreements with Joshua Nkomo. ZANU is officially recognized as a liberation movement by the Organisation of African Unity and the United Nations.

Many ZANU leaders have been restricted and imprisoned for political offences. Ndabaningi Sithole was in prison or restriction from 1964 until December 1974. ZANU itself was banned on 26 August 1964. ZANU guerillas have been active inside Rhodesia since UDI especially in the north-east; they were responsible for the first post-UDI action at Sinoia.

ZANU was a signatory to the unity agreement reached in Lusaka in December 1974 under which the four African nationalist organisations (ZANU, ZAPU, FROLIZI and the ANC) united in the re-constituted African National Council.

52.

What is the African National Council (ANC)?

The ANC, involving members of both ZAPU and ZANU, was founded in December 1971 to organize a united campaign for the rejection of the Home-Smith settlement proposals. It successfully co-ordinated opposition despite many obstructive actions by the Smith regime prior to and during the test of acceptability by the Pearce Commission.

The ANC continued to " struggle for national emancipation from the yoke of a racist and oppressive minority rule " despite the detention of many of its leaders during the post-Pearce period.

In the summer of 1973 discussions commenced between the Smith regime and the ANC in an attempt to reach " an internal settlement " but in June 1974 proposals put forward

by the Smith regime were unanimously rejected. Following
the detention of Dr. Edson Sithole, an ANC leader, later in
June the ANC suspended all talks with the Smith regime.

In November and December 1974 the ANC was represented
in talks in Lusaka, Zambia involving ZAPU, ZANU and the
Heads of State of Zambia, Tanzania and Botswana. Following
these talks the African nationalist organisations, ZAPU,
ZANU and FROLIZI agreed to merge into the re-constituted
ANC.

<h3 align="center">53.</h3>

Which African nationalist organisations have been banned, and when?

Successive African nationalist organizations have been banned
whenever they have appeared to be a serious threat to the
continuation of white minority rule. Since World War II the
main ones have been as follows:
● African National Congress of Southern Rhodesia:
Formed 12.9.1957; Banned 25.2.1959.
● National Democratic Party: Formed 1.1.1960; Banned
9.12.1961.
● Zimbabwe African People's Union: Formed 17.12.1961;
Banned 19.9.1962.
● Zimbabwe African National Union: Formed 8.8.1963;
Banned 26.8.1964.
● People's Caretaker Council: Formed 10.8.1963; Banned
26.8.1964.

<h3 align="center">54.</h3>

Why has the African liberation movement not always been united?

The struggle for a free and democratic Zimbabwe has at times
been weakened by the disagreements which have occurred
between the African nationalist organisations. But it is
important not to forget the many areas of common policy

which they have; nor to ignore the factors which have given rise to disagreements.

The two major nationalist organisations prior to the Lusaka unity agreement (December 1974) ZAPU and ZANU have been agreed both on their objectives, majority rule and a democratic Zimbabwe, and also on the means to achieve this—the use of armed struggle. Their willingness to co-operate was revealed in their decision to establish a Joint Military Command in March 1972 and a Joint Political Council in March 1973.

The original cause of the split in the summer of 1963 was disagreements within the ZAPU leadership. Without commenting in detail on these disagreements it is possible to explain some of the factors which gave rise to them:

● the fact that all other British colonies had been successful in negotiating independence led to high expectations that independence under majority rule was nigh;

● the continued banning of nationalist organisations and the detention and restriction of nationalist leaders made it very difficult to organise an effective movement;

● there was uncertainty as to whether and how to effect a transition from peaceful to armed struggle.

These differences regarding timing and methods, together with personality clashes during this period, left a mark on the nationalist movement but at the same time the desire for unity persisted.

The agreement reached in Lusaka in December 1974 between ZAPU, ZANU, FROLIZI and the ANC suggests that the old disagreements have been overcome. New ones may emerge, but this is to be expected in the course of the evolution and growth of any political movement.

55.

Guerilla activity has been reported in Rhodesia. How extensive and effective has it been?

Guerilla units of ZAPU and ZANU have been operating inside Rhodesia since UDI. Both liberation movements had decided that armed stuggle was inevitable both because the Smith regime was preventing any peaceful resistance to its policies and because the British government had failed to intervene to prevent UDI.

The first post-UDI action was at Sinoia in April 1966. Sporadic guerilla attacks continued until mid-1967 when joint units of ZAPU and the African National Congress of South Africa launched a major campaign in the Wankie region which lasted for several months. The Smith regime had to appeal to South Africa for assistance. In August 1967 South African para-military units arrived in Rhodesia. (See Question 59).

After mid-1972 guerilla activity reached a new level of effectiveness with sustained actions throughout north and north-east Rhodesia. This appears to have been a major factor in the desire of the Rhodesian and South African regimes to reach a settlement.

Following talks in Lusaka in November and December an informal ceasefire was announced pending the convening of a Constitutional Conference.

56.

What has been the response of the Smith regime to this guerilla activity?

The Smith regime has been compelled to mount and sustain a large and ever-growing operation in an attempt to contain the guerilla activity. Measures taken include:
- large increases in military and security expenditure;
- the creation of " no go " areas and the forced removal of thousands of Africans into so-called " protected villages ";
- The construction of a security network of roads and communications using forced labour;
- The closure of schools, businesses etc., the seizure of cattle, imposition of collective fines, and the introduction of curfews in affected areas.

Captured guerillas have been tortured and imprisoned; many have been hanged following secret trials. Over a hundred Africans have been imprisoned for the offence of " failing to report terrorists ".

How large is Rhodesia's military budget?

Planned military expenditure (army and airforce) for the year 1974-5 was R$46.2 million, compared with R$19.3 million for 1970-71.

Police expenditure has also increased dramatically. Projected expenditure for 1974-5 being R$31.2 million compared with R$15.4 million for 1970-1.

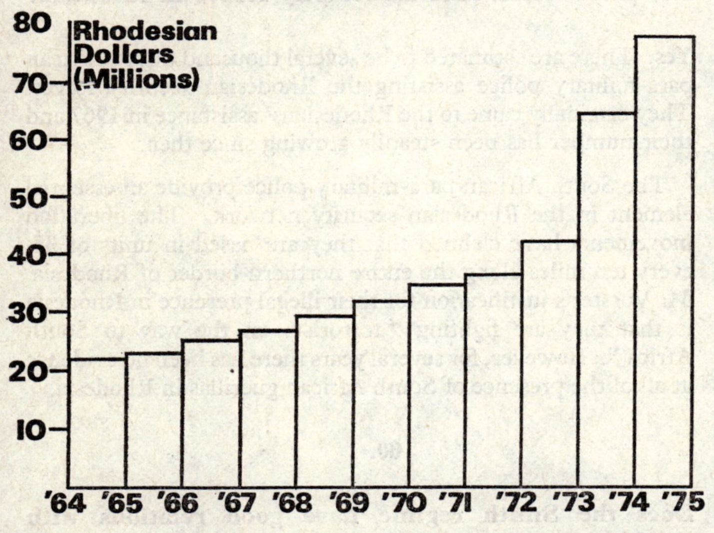

Fig 5. Security Expenditure, 1964/5 — 1974/5. (Defence & Police Votes)

58.

Is there military service in Rhodesia?

Yes, all white male Rhodesians on reaching the age of 18 are required to complete one year of national service in the army, airforce, police or the Ministry of Internal Affairs. Men who have completed their national service or who are over 25 are registered as Territorials or reservists.

Since December 1972 there have been repeated call-ups of Territorials and reservists. The frequency of these call-ups is reported to be having serious effects on the economy; many men have been required to serve four 28-day tours of duty within a period of 14 months.

59.

Are there South African security forces in Rhodesia?

Yes. There are estimated to be several thousand South African para-military police assisting the Rhodesian security forces. They originally came to the Rhodesians' assistance in 1967 and their number has been steadily growing since then.

The South African para-military police provide an essential element in the Rhodesian security network. The liberation movements have claimed that they are based in units of 35, every ten miles along the entire northern border of Rhodesia. Mr Vorster's justification for their illegal presence in Rhodesia is that they are fighting " terrorists on the way to South Africa ". However, for several years there has been no evidence at all of the presence of South African guerillas in Rhodesia.

60.

Does the Smith regime have good relations with neighbouring countries?

The map on page 20 shows that Rhodesia borders on Zambia, Botswana, Mozambique and South Africa. The character of Rhodesia's relations with these four states differs considerably.
ZAMBIA:
Rhodesia has no diplomatic relations with Zambia and since

the closure of the Rhodesia/Zambia border in 1972 their (formerly extensive) trade and other economic relations have become virtually non-existent.

There have been frequent reports of incursions by the Rhodesian security forces into Zambian territory and air-space. In 1973 the Zambian Minister of Defence announced that there had been 100 such incursions since 1965 and that 20 Zambians had been killed.

BOTSWANA:

Relations between Botswana and Rhodesia have been tense ever since Botswana gained its independence in 1966. No formal diplomatic relations exist but because of Botswana's relative isolation from independent Africa certain economic relations have continued. The railway line through Botswana, one of Rhodesia's main links with South Africa, is still owned by Rhodesia Railways although the Botswana government has declared its intention to take it over.

MOZAMBIQUE:

Prior to April 1974 Rhodesia maintained good relations with the Portuguese authorities in Mozambique. Rhodesian security forces assisted the Portuguese army in their war against FRELIMO, the Mozambique liberation movement; the Rhodesians benefited from extensive assistance in sanctions breaking by the Portuguese. All this is likely to change when Mozambique is independent under FRELIMO leadership.

SOUTH AFRICA:

Rhodesia and South Africa have developed very close relations since UDI. South Africa has assisted Rhodesia militarily, economically (especially in sanctions breaking) and in the diplomatic field. Rhodesia has consequently become increasingly dependent on South Africa. Following the revolution in Portugal in April 1974 the construction of a direct rail link between South Africa and Rhodesia was speeded up and completed.

This dependence on South Africa by the Rhodesian regime has enabled the South African government to exert considerable influence which it used in November and December 1974 to persuade the Rhodesian authorities to allow leading nationalist detainees to visit Lusaka, Zambia for talks.

61.

What are the main sectors of the Rhodesian economy?

The main sectors of the economy are:

- **Agriculture:**   Chief products include cotton, tobacco, beef and maize;
- **Mining:**   Main minerals include asbestos, chrome, nickel, coal, iron and gold;
- **Manufacturing:**   Mainly light and heavy industry, foodstuffs and textiles;
- **Tourism:**   Tourist centres include Victoria Falls, Kariba, Wankie game reserve and Zimbabwe ruins.

62.

What are UN mandatory sanctions?

The United Nations imposed comprehensive mandatory sanctions against Rhodesia because it regards the situation in Rhodesia as a "threat to peace and security". Any member state of the UN which imports Rhodesian goods or exports goods to Rhodesia, except for a number of specified products which are exempted for humanitarian reasons, is acting in violation of Article 25 of the UN Charter.

Mandatory sanctions were initially introduced in December 1966 but only on a selective basis. They were made comprehensive in May 1968. (The original UN sanctions against Rhodesia introduced on 20 November 1965 were purely voluntary in character).

The UN Security Council has established a Sanctions Committee which receives reports of sanctions breaking and requires member states involved to explain or take action in such cases.

63.

What effect have they had on Rhodesia?

The Rhodesian economy has managed to withstand the imposition of both voluntary and mandatory UN sanctions. It is able to sell all its major exports and through South Africa to import most essential goods. It has also been able to raise large sums for investment on the international capital market.

Sanctions have led to many shortages and have had a distorting effect on the Rhodesian economy and so to that extent they have contributed to the weakening of white minority rule.

Sanctions, however, have not brought about the collapse of the illegal Smith regime nor have they achieved the British government's initial aim of dividing the white community.

The roles played by South Africa, which has continued "normal trading relations", and the Portuguese in Mozambique, who assisted in sanction-breaking operations, have been crucial in preventing the effective implementation of sanctions.

64.

Which countries have been the main offenders against UN sanctions?

South Africa and Portugal have blatantly defied all UN resolutions relating to Rhodesia. However many other countries have been continuing trading relations with Rhodesia. They include the United States which explicitly allows the importing of chrome and other strategic minerals and Switzerland, a non-member of the UN, which has maintained trade with Rhodesia at pre-UDI levels.

Exposures of sanctions-breaking operations have revealed that countries such as Japan, the Netherlands, Greece and West Germany have also been trading with Rhodesia.

65.

What has Britain's role been in the imposition of sanctions?

Britain's role has been the subject of much criticism from

African states particularly for its action in vetoing resolutions at the United Nations Security Council which were designed to tighten sanctions.

The British government made it clear immediately after UDI that sanctions were not designed to overthrow the Smith regime but to persuade it to return to legality. Nor did it want sanctions to bring it into conflict with South Africa.

These factors explain why for two and a half years after UDI the British government prevented the UN Security Council from imposing comprehensive mandatory sanctions. This delay provided the Smith regime with sufficient time to devise numerous means of evading sanctions.

Since the introduction of mandatory comprehensive sanctions Britain together with other Western governments has prevented any effective action by the UN against the two major sanctions-breaking states, South Africa and Portugal.

66.

Which countries have diplomatic relations with Rhodesia?

None; but in two countries, South Africa and Portugal, Rhodesia maintains diplomatic representatives.

FURTHER READING

Ideas for further reading are suggested in the list below. Some of the publications are no longer in print but should be available from a good reference library.

IDAF Pamphlets

Why Minority Rule Survives (1969, 40pp). Useful summary of white rule in Rhodesia; contains details of both the *Tiger* and *Fearless* proposals.

The British Dilemma by E. E. Mlambo (1970, 37pp). Includes description of repressive legislation and labour laws; also summary of 1969 Constitution.

The White Judge's Burden by Mervyn Jones (1972, 25pp). An account of the events surrounding the Pearce Commission's visit to Rhodesia.

South Africa's Sixth Province by John Sprack (1974, 88pp). Deals primarily with Rhodesia's links with South Africa, but contains much useful information on land, labour, education and the economy.

Other Pamphlets

A Principle in Torment published by the United Nations (1969, 71pp). Detailed account of UN action on Rhodesia.

From Rhodesia to Zimbabwe by Kees Maxey published by the Fabian Society (1972, 40pp). An account of African resistance to white rule.

No Future Without Us published by E. E. Mlambo (1972, 48pp). The story of the African National Council in Zimbabwe.

Books

The Struggle for a Birthright by Eshmael Mlambo published by C. Hurst, London. (1972, 332pp).

Crisis in Rhodesia by Nathan Shamuyarira published by Andre Deutsch. (1965, 240pp).

Zimbabwe Now published by Rex Collings (1973, 142pp).

The Right To Say No by Judith Todd published by Sidgwick and Jackson (1972, 200pp).

U.D.I. by Robert C. Good published by Faber and Faber, (1973, 368pp).

Specialist Studies

The Rhodesia—Zambia border closure, Jan-Feb. 1973, IDAF (1973).

The Fight for Zimbabwe: The armed conflict in Southern Rhodesia, by Kees Maxey, published by Rex Collings Ltd. (1975).

Insurgency in Rhodesia, 1957-73: An Account and Assessment by A. R. Wilkinson published by the International Institute for Strategic Studies (1974).

Revolt in Southern Rhodesia, 1896-7 by T. O. Ranger published by Heinemann Educational (1967).

The Character and Legislation of the Rhodesian Front since UDI by Reg Austin published by the Africa Bureau (1968).

The 'Fearless' Proposals and the Six Principles by M. J. Christie published by the Africa Bureau (1968).

Rhodesia: Report of the Commission on Rhodesian Opinion under the chairmanship of the Right Honourable the Lord Pearce Cmnd 4964 published by HMSO (1972).

Information Service

The Southern Africa Information Service (Vols 1-4) published by IDAF contains a detailed record of events in Rhodesia.

Printed by A. G. Bishop & Sons Ltd., Orpington, Kent